T0063318

FAILING MATHS AND MY OTHER CRIMES

ALSO BY THABO JIJANA

Nobody's Business (Jacana Media, 2014)

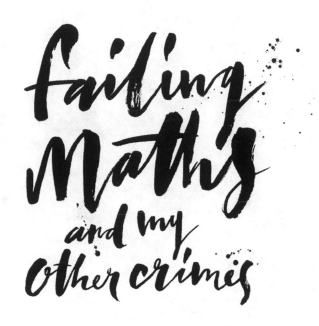

failing Maths and my other crimes

POEMS BY

THABO JIJANA

UHLANGA NEW POETS

2015

Failing Maths and My Other Crimes
Part of the uHlanga New Poets series
© Thabo Jijana, 2015, all rights reserved

Published in Cape Town, South Africa by uHlanga in 2015
uhlangapress.co.za

Distributed outside South Africa by African Books Collective
africanbookscollective.com

ISBN: 978-0-620-67693-9

Cover image by Nick Mulgrew
Cover illustration by Alice Edy

The body text of this book is set at 10pt/15pt in Didot HTF 11.

ACKNOWLEDGEMENTS

The first versions of some of the poems in this book originally
appeared in the following magazines, websites and anthologies:
New Contrast, the *Kalahari Review*, *Poetry Potion*, *The Sol Plaatje
European Union Poetry Anthology Vol. IV* (Jacana Media, 2014),
uHlanga, and *Black Communion (Poems of The New African Poets)*
(Wale Owoade, 2014). The author would like to thank the editors of
each of these publications.

The author would also like to acknowledge the sources and partial
sources of the following poems:

- "Mfana wam" is a translation from isiXhosa of a poem by the same name by
L. M. S. Ngewabe, originally published in *Khala Zome* (Bona Press, 1965).
- "Calabash" is a found poem taken from an op-ed by SEK Mqhayi,
"Wolokohlo Kwelimnyama", from *Izwi Labantu*, (September 17, 1901), with
translation by Phyllis Ntantala.
- A fragment of "Nandi's smile" was taken from *History in Action* (Juta and
Co., 1987), a high school textbook edited by DL Davel, HA Schreuder, and
E Engelbrecht.
- "Homelessness" is a found poem, based on a quote by Vivienne
Westwood, recorded in *Time* (January 14, 2009).
- "Botswana blues" is a found poem, based on a passage from *A Woman
Alone: Autobiographical Writings* by Bessie Head (African Writers Series,
Heinemann Publishers, 1990).
- "Mabuya'mbo" is a found poem, based on a passage from "Amasiko
nezithethe neendlela zokuziphatha kwaXhosa", an MA dissertation by
Zodwa Geingea-Ndolo (Unisa, 2008).

The publication of this book was made possible due partly to a grant
by Nedbank Arts Affinity through the Arts & Culture Trust. uHlanga
would like to express their gratitude to both institutions.

CONTENTS

To my father, once more

You have no power here

I will tell you what I know.
It won't be what you want me to tell you,
or what you think I should know.
Not what is written down for the children to imbibe;
not the story of Nongqawuse, that swayable girl
wandering around the Cape wild, leading Phalo's sons
Qamata knows where.

I will tell you what I know.
It won't be what those who do you dirty
will want me to say.
It won't be nice.
It won't be like wine.
It won't be broadcast delayed live on the speaking box.

I will tell you what I know.
Sticks and stone, burning tyres,
Andries Tatane, that man they killed in Alex.
Did you ever hear what was said
on June 26, 1953, a year after the Defiance Campaign
had begun in Port Elizabeth?
That every parent must tell their children
about the campaign and the sacrifices
the people had made?

Where were you when "Zandisile" came out?
The One Love Movement on Bantu Biko Street?
I will tell you where: glued to your couch,
no more moved by the visuals on eNCA
than when you suffered a lesson
on the bitter fruits of the French Revolution,
and how it left behind the impression
that violence ought to be legalised
as a method of maintaining order;
that an individual's life was of less importance
than the objectives of the group in control.

I will tell you what mam'Nywabe used to tell me:
to always pick fruit from the lowest branches,
for if the tree wanted you to have it all,
it would forget about the primates and drop down
all its fruits 'til the ground in all the gardens
were covered with every type of produce.

I will tell you what I know.
I will tell you everything I know.
Give me a moment,
and I shall begin.

Calabash

To be in charge of
    this skin calabash
        into which
    to pour our hopes,
wishes and aspirations;

a calabash that
    would give us
        a beverage
    that would not
sour the stomach

of the offspring of the braves
    and notables
        of our land,
    causing wind
in their stomachs.

Monkey's wedding

As for me, I had taken the forefeet,
hands as manacles about the hooves,
not that Nana, my goat –
         flat on her back,
         legs spread apart,
her own angora pelt
a foam mattress –
could object
from where she rested.

Cousin Wele had one knee on the dung floor
beside the gaping abdomen,
scooping the entrails
         onto a metal washbasin.

I didn't know the sun could get so hot that
it rained tears, but Wele did not like to hear me
say foolish things,
so I swallowed the singing of my heart
as I had the tears in my eyes
when tata rung a rope
around Nana's neck
and yanked her to where she was now.

It was pleasant to watch the soft dance
of raindrops
hopping on the tin sheet
that had been laid on the floor.

It was pleasant to feel the sunshine
warm my moist, bare back.

Somewhere about the cattle kraal, I heard tata
call out my name. He said to bring a cooking pot
for the offal. "Now."
My legs felt numb. "And stop
                being so slow."

I walked out, then I walked back in
to find Wele chopping the body
with a machete,
and I saw that it was hard work.

The Latter-Day Saints are here

The family was alerted quite early
of the arrival by tooth ferry
of the festal chirrun
    who – with the verve of Marabi,
the unity of imanyano,
and the smoothness of mieliepap –
arrived one by one, two by two.
    Soon as my son's gums started to itch
we knew the habitués had pitched,
and the first two we christened
Bongani and Mawande,
    to say, "We are thankful,"
and, "May many more follow."

In all this dryness of a bitchy life,
nothing beats watching the young ones
helm forward the ship,
    for even growing teeth
has taken on a higher feat.

We must be thankful,
we must.

Domkop

A sore heart brings to mind an open wound that
is the consequence
of some mishap with a Minora blade, gaping
like the corner of a reliable suitcase
torn at the seam
in some freak accident the bus conductor
forgot to tell you about
after loading your luggage,
leaving exposed some things it would do well
not to draw a stranger's eye to.
You don't want to have to explain the strip
of Elastoplast on your chin,
as though you can't hold a shaving razor properly.
It isn't a nice thing
to befall one – yes.
It's shameful
to talk about – maybe.
Hence you laugh it away
much like when you clutch your belongings
tight under the armpit,
making light of the conductor's crime
long after you've disembarked from the bus.

Children watching old people

malume drinks
the last of his chibuku beer
as though he were
knocking out
bone marrow,
hitting the carton
        violently
against the
palm of his hand
& licking
        the score
noisily

Mfana wam

My son, this life will come to pass.
When nightfall greets you, be glad each of your breaths
has been spent by way of solid labour in pursuit
    of a restful subsistence.

Those who reach the hilltop of the life we live
have marched through the hardships we know
and bear the scars and heartache
    to prove it.

True manhood cannot be bought or forged,
the only way to attain it is to learn how to be a man
the hard way. This I liken to gold: through great toil it is dug and honed
    'til its very importance is realised.

Like your mother's most precious gourd slipping off your fingers
and hitting the ground hard, your brain will come undone:
To spend all your youth learning and learning is no amusement.
    This I know, but it must be done.

There will always be days when nothing is ever good,
but there will be a moment, every now and again,
when triumph and delight
    shall return to your heart.

In this our beggarly world, there is hardly incentive to lead
a just life. Still, you must try to bring honour upon your father's name.
Give your all, walk tall, and speak strong – you are our hope,
   my son.

Urgent situation

Outside the grocer,
an old man in overalls,
searching his pockets.

Nandi's smile

His mother had been driven away
from his father's dwelling
when he was but still crawling. Romance issues.
(I'll leave it to you
to fill in the missing years.)
Upon her death
in 1827
he ordered a public mourning, and if
his people did not display sufficient grief
they were executed on the spot.
To evidence their sorrow they were ordered
to undertake no cultivation, and the milk of the cows
was to be spilled on the ground – all of which
brought untold suffering
on the people.

Nodumehlezi: the one who makes the earth rumble
when he sits.
You call him Shaka. You might as well accept
that he was General My Way, that he was – yes,
you got it: Mr Only.

Loinfruits

They all had a hand
in his fall. "O, children
of my father! What have
I ever done
to you?"
A lot, actually.

Adam Kok III as man of sorrow

In a museum,
children face his likeness,
talk of history.

Biko

all is dead
but for the
mosquitoes
singing
their blood song

my shirt wet
as a dishrag

*he slept most
of the way*

in my foldaway
wheelchair
behind the bars
they funnel past,
kitskonstabels
carrying a stretcher
of blankets
like a sack
of mielie-mielie,
& deliver
        the naked man
to the "discussed
destination"

welcome to the
knacker's yard

when they stopped
for petrol
he was not given
a chance to get
out to stretch
his legs

this is what
to think: he's
a dead man
now

they pick on your
brain so your head is
like Swiss cheese
with holes leaking
your sanity
everywhere

he was not
a doctor and
could not say
whether the
man was in
a state
of collapse

to remain calm
for him;
soon, things
wouldn't
be

a black man, he
was on his own

irresponsible people
from Coca-Cola &
hamburger cultural
backgrounds,
they were
on their own

a bottle of water
by way
of equipment,
a bed that consists
of a mat
in the corner
of the cell

*he could not
answer back
when
the white man
visited him*

alone
he lay on
the stone floor

alone

The Will and Testament of Brenda Fassie

Quite the opposite: going
to bed with one eye open, living
came to seem
                    an accident
of fate.

Banana moon

To see this story better, close your eyes
and picture a mud village,
safely hidden in a quiet valley.
There is the sort of beat-up sedan
that passes for a short-distance taxicab
parked near the kraal;
it is late on a Saturday evening,
and now a banana of a moon
casts a cloak of dim light
over the proceedings

– that takes care of the where.

The what is the thing that took place
on the heels of auntie Nokwakha's funeral,
where I remember uncle Mncedi weep
and laugh
just a little
in front of a tentful of attendees,
stopping every now and then
to wipe his tears
with a handkerchief
some alert female mourner upfront
had handed him.
The first time
in my twenty-odd years

I had seen uncle Mncedi –
a keen public speaker
and reigning champ
of dining-room raconteuring –
lose his composure.
The only time
I would ever see a man
of my family
conduct himself
this way.

When, how, why – forget all that.

I won't say my cousins weren't having fun.
The five of them piled into Nyaniso's jalopy,
to each man his own glass.
It was there, I suspect, that they carried out
their aftertears,
a tippler's caucus
on a cold August.

I was the who this night – the omission.
Too young with the bottle. No vrou.
So I hung back.

This was before I had matured enough
to detest the modern black funeral;
how it is treated as though
it were another traditional ceremony:
comparable only to a birthday party
with a guest of honour

whose presence
is only a grainy ID photo
enlarged on a piece of paper.

Some days I wonder to myself
if it had occurred at all
to any of my brothers
to ask themselves
whether they drank Castle Lite
to dull their pain,
or maybe because
they had merely acquired
a shared affection
for funerals
the way some people
love public holidays:

for the festive vigils
that go on and on
and on and on
after the burial
at the tavern.

Mabuya'mbo

Yayilisiko lamaXhosa
ukubona nje umfazi wamathile
enkxuza umbona emanzini,
elungiselela ukwenza imbiza,
ukusila utywala, ukwenzela ukuba
indoda yalapha kweli khaya
ikhe ibize iingwevu zakowayo
zikhe zize kutshica
kweli khaya lazo.
Ibisenziwa ke le nto kungekho
nto imbi, kungalilwa,
kungafiwanga
koko konwatyiwe.

Kodwa kule mihla xa kufuneka kwenziwe
njengoko kwakusaya kwenziwa,
uya kuva umfazi weli khaya ekhalaza,
ekhalazela ukuba umzi wakhe uyangcoliswa
ngaba bantu baza kube belapho emzini.

Homelessness

The nearest
      I've ever come to it
was going home
      and finding
I didn't have
      my door key
with me.

Serowe's daughter

Let us assume she got off at the train station in Palapye, dressed
tastefully as only a black lady in the sixties could, and beside her she
was clasping the hand of her son as they went about looking for the
bus. Let us assume it was a warm March day and that they found
their way to Serowe, then a village in central Botswana, without
much trouble. She was 27. He was 2.

It is said she was happy, having finally left South Africa, though fearful
of what awaited her on this journey. Still, someone from the
Tshekedi Khama Memorial Primary School, where she would soon
be teaching, must have met her on her arrival in the village and
showed her to the hut in Sebina ward, near the centre of Serowe,
where she would stay. Another time, she must have taken a moment
to register her new neighbourhood: hedged by a set of low hills
on one side, a community of sprawling mud huts, the walls of the
Batswana villagers' courtyards decorated with elaborate patterns of
colour, a "heavy, rich smell of breathing earth everywhere."

There seems to be little confusion on the surface of life, she would later
remark in writing. *There is a sense of wovenness, a wholeness in
life here; a feeling of how strange and beautiful people can be – just
living.*

Botswana blues

I have learnt bitterly
and deeply
that some things
    are beyond my control.
I am simply victimised by them
and there is no such thing
    as saying
God help me.

The thing about Mugabe

young men
in baseball caps
& golf shirts,
with fake leather purses
heaving like a bunch
of clown's balloons
on both arms,
hawking
door to door
without any shame.

the township, Motherwell:
on a street
Zimbabwean bagmen shuffle
past a shanty
with a rickety postern
& Lucky Dube
at max volume
and, in the vanishing
light
of dusk,
a crooked tree
casting thin shadows
on the front yard.

they pass through life
like orphans & runaways:
their days
a prophesy disbelieved
but never forgotten.

they cannot escape
the bemused look.

Currency

The Zaire is not some exotic dance
originally glimpsed amidst
          the liberation crusades
of the 1970s, when a black man
          with a Muslim name
could call Africa the jungle
and declare himself its king.
No, no – *if you who no know*
                    go know.

Spilling blood

I pray I never take to poetry
as some people go to church
to run away from the things
                          on the street:
the loud music played from the boots
of trendy cars
at the gumba-gumba that everyone
will talk about
                          on Sunday morning
when morning service is over and a story
spreads through the township
                          that a girl barely with breasts
slept with an older man
by the toilets
                          at the back of the tavern
and that, of course, someone with a cellphone
                          videoed every moment of it.

I hope for my poetry to be empirical.
It shall suggest making love:
you will want the usual
                          in an unusual way.
It ought to remind one
of the house song
                          that says:
"I am ready to spill blood
for my man."

Old Spice

Let's say you hear a Bheki Mseleku record
– *as I did, last night* – and your mind drifts
to an image of her face, silent and waiting,
as one meets the tired stare of the taxi driver
You were in love with her, weren't you?
on the rearview mirror

                                while surveying traffic.
You may decide – as I did, this morning – that
people who don't know the answers
must learn to keep quiet.

So what, you both agreed to friendship as a parting gift?
At the time you needed her most.
Sure, the memory of your love then
seems to give the air hands even today,

                          such that
your heart on gravy,
the wind cupped under your toes,

                          you touch
                          the sky.

Yodeler of Painful Laughs (an appraisal: Brenda F.)

She was
(as divas go)
into other people,
and people were
(as radio minds go)
into her.

Baby

At a knees-up once, I met this girl –
already a ripening frump,
and I thought
if I looked hard enough, I may well see
her gogo, chewing tobacco and carping.

That same day, voodoo hours, moonlight
peering in from the big window
that looked out onto the backyard
of my dwelling then,
shadows peeking behind the chair,
chest of drawers and wardrobe.

Baby, she said
with pretentious interest.

No one can blame me
for turning and looking
the other way, pretending
to finish my drink
                and placing the dumpy
atop the bedside table.

It must be that I knew there and then,
how hard it must be
to get rid of bad people in your life.
Not them resisting,
but you not realising

that you should have never
befriended them in the first place,
nor the need
to take a look
at your people every once
in a while
and let go
of those who are
dead weight.

        I can't recall
if she ever gave me her real name.

The glorious history of Adam's apple

If he stopped mid-swallow and let
the apple fall to his feet, the other hand raised
to his neck – a man strangling
himself – it cannot be that Adam
had caught glimpse of the snake pastor
hard at work, performing miracles.
It could only be that the un-chewed piece
lodged in his throat
was giving him a lot of trouble.

Watching Grandfather's small, quiet eyes after Grandmother's burial

Lips ajar, words leaking out
to gather on the base of the teacup
he cradles on his lap. On his head
a frayed cap, the rest of him
a background to a blur of gestures.
Let me tell you! Sweetness
walks with bitterness.

Mandela spent half his life in one room,
or it must have felt like it on that
first step,
his feet planted on the
tarmac outside the gates at Victor Verster.
Winnie at one hand; the other a raised fist.

He must have wanted to scream,

or loosen his tie and dance. It's a
pity we'll never know.

Everybody loves the sunshine

Outside a shack,
two young men on stools,
soccer on the radio.

Amadou and Mariam

You must have despised me for wanting you,
though this may yet absolve me as fool:
witness how I brood over the good love
loitering, long after we ceased to hug!

No, we cannot be as the bourgeoisie
when we live and die still as farmyard pigs.
But was I not a man taking the stand
to be a simple and proud African?

With you I was assured we had been spawned
from some place of safety far beyond Earth;
nowhere where a supposed given shall
alter as suddenly as the heavens.

Such mephitic unrest has ailed this chest –
here I now promise to ail someone else.

Evidence of things known but not understood

I remember that I received it
with the quietism
deserving of things sacrosanct
– no more than wisdom
        gained after a puff of the herb.
First I found the spade,
then came back
and slid it beneath the millipede.
It curled into a question mark,
        then a smooth coil. I knew
then that I had been quite scared
by the creature. Why had I affected
otherwise?
Obviously I still want to
discern
the lesson I forgot
        to learn then – badly.

But understand: I was young.

Sweet nothings

It's not that I trade
in acts of sweet talk,
of boomerangs, its very name
a children's lullaby.

Not as bowed
        as a C
or elongated
        as rhino horn,
or enraged
        as sporting wood.

To all those bumptious
men with briefcases slipping
on their yellow peels
and falling over,
        occiput first,
on the sidewalk:

I bring only requests
for clemency.

The thing about Manto and beetroot

Car lights flash past the
windows and soon I expect
him to walk through the door,
saying hello. Tonight he'll be tired,
stinking of engine fumes, the
sleeves of his corduroy shirt
rolled up to the elbow, his hands
caked with oil. Whatever's
in the plastic bag he'll be clutching,
Sisi will bring to us: she's
the oldest child, and as we all sit
around the TV, she'll divide
the Simbas and raisins or
the honey popcorn so that all
three of us boys have equal
share. She will keep the
biggest share for herself.
When are you taking us to
town? I will ask soon. *You've*
been promising. And if I
close my eyes, I can see him
through the archway, looking
up from his plate of chicken
liver and rice at the kitchen
table. He'll tell me to go wash
the van clean first, then we can
talk. I can hear the sound of

the tablespoon hitting that
ceramic plate – he is a fast
eater – as I pull the door
behind me and look in the
direction of our zinc-sheet
garage. But I know tonight
is not a night he comes
home. Not since the men
dug a deep hole beside the kraal,
where there is now a dune
of red soil and a white cross;
the black paint washed away,
nothing as clean as a name.

Making a scene

Somewhere in a squatter camp,
a door yawned open and a man
appeared at the doorstep, silhouetted
as only the faint light coming from outside
alerted the mosquito quietly
gliding past him into the house.
                              If by
any misfortune of sorcery, you had
been transmuted to a small person
on the back of that mosquito, holding
onto its fine hair with your small
arms, you would see the man raise a
hand to his mouth and retrieve a broken
tibia bone from the drumstick he was
chewing, throw it out on the sandy
ground before him and pick up a
chicken wing from the smeared
plate he held with his other hand.
                              You would
hear a woman's voice going, "Quickly
my love, the mosquitos." Too late, you
would think. By now the man will be
chewing the last bits of the bones.
He will spit the bits onto his hand
and throw out that too. And just as
he turns to go into the house, he will
hear growling, low and steady,
then some chomping.

"They're at it
again," he will say for the woman's benefit.
"Who?" the woman will say. "MamNgwe's
dogs." More chomping. "They're quick,
those two." Quicker than an ambulance,
you'll want to say. But, of course, the man
and woman would have not yet heard the two
of you come in through the door.

Failing maths and my other crimes

An epistle in free verse isn't as easy as it looks, especially when
you want
to address your younger self.
You would think all you need
is a "Dear friend"
and a "How are you?" for your work to be half done.
But even I admit
       I could scarcely explain myself
now,
never mind
the boy who came out of that reading room
a new man,
safe in the hope of what was to come
in the summers of his life.

February the month, a Valentine's theme
at the library.
It was the kind of sunny afternoon that were Jesus
to saunter through the foyer, hardcovers weighing
under the armpit,
the surplice of his trade
billowing out behind him.
I wouldn't have thought to call him out
and ask
where he had been
       all these years.
I needed something to believe in –
my thoughts would be elsewhere.

"Friend of my zodiac," I find myself
writing down, "how goes you there, sani?"

I wouldn't be so impulsive as to call it the sum
of my rap sheet –
failing maths in secondary school
        and my other crimes afterwards –
but bills have come due and dues must be paid:

I remember liking the title, *Bury Me at the Marketplace*,
and remember too the bottom half of page 104.
There was the gladness in the author's words
as though my heart
was the object of their aim.
I imagined an old man at the kitchen table,
a lone candle and the dead light bulb dangling
        above his balding head
the only witnesses to his pastime.
I remember still thinking of my own father,
the image of him in his cardigan and torn jeans
the last time we spoke
at the taxi rank.

And then came the moment I thought: but oh,
are they not loving
to me,
these men,
and these words?

I said you need people more than you think, that
I hoped we could work towards

a healthier relationship; that
my restriction was not absolute
but instead grew
           out of your attitude.

         "Parents,"
he lectured the letter-writer
to his daughter,
         "are fixtures
like all the planets."

Parents don't orbit.
It's the young who orbit,
like the satellites and asteroids,
and so it is them who must return
to the fixtures.

There came the moment I stepped out and into the sunlight
and knew it in my heart what it was
that I wanted:
to be comfortable in the knowledge of my pain
at my father's passing
and to trust in the tomorrow and its promise
of the antidote.

I have learnt to taste the seasons
         of my life
as only my tongue is able: to take the sweet
and the sour without discriminating against
the bitter and the salty.

Soon each new visit to the fitting room
at the clothing shop
will be for me an exercise
        in the physiological revelation that defines aging.
But I've never been so sure
and as trusting as I am now in the knowledge that the measure
of my maturity
is that I can love again.

We are all orbits of some sort,
circling around the world we call our own,
        and literature...
Literature is a compass;
it helped me find myself that afternoon
on Govan Mbeki Avenue,
stuffed as I was in a woollen jersey and slacks.
Though fitting, those garments were in that moment
for a young man clashing with the elements of his world;
a young man too tired
        to care any longer.

Nothing is worth fighting for anymore
but love and joy in your heart.

"Just a note
        to say hello,"
is how my letter goes,
        finally,
"and to say welcome
to this new summer.
        That is all."

Sprinkling ashes

This is not an ode about home, where the grass is tall
and the hills are green, where the rivers are full
and ever potent; where the girls are to cherish and the young
men never tire of answering to the riddles of manhood. What

might you be like had you seen him spun around
as though a hurried hawker had bumped him from behind,
only to greet his own shadow, bedecked in the same
ill-fitting coat and khakis, toenails poking like prying eyes

from his toe rags? The quiet silhouettes of others whirled
past him, trampling on his clone. He stooped, as if to clasp
the hand of his shadow, then retreated. A deceitful glimmer burnished
below just as his double mimed his hobble. *If you travel,*

you see things with your own eyes. This is an ode about
the marketplaces of Africa, where many of my people
endure daily, trying, struggling, failing, trying yet again
to make it to another Monday.

Kindly remember

Take the town dogs, for instance. They hang around
among the caravans looking for chewed bones or garbage,
ownerless, fending for their own skinny selves, being
beat up by the vagrants when they encroach
on their turf.

Take the police officer walking in the direction of his favourite
mobile café. Wait until he reaches the door and says, *Where were you
when I wanted a wife?* That's his greeting. Then he'll make
a sound as if he can just tell how delicious the day's special is
from the aromas that greet him. *Mmmmm-mmm*, he will say
loud enough so everyone nearby can hear. *Mmmmm-mmm*, he will say,
with a cheerful smile you have never seen before.

Take the young women near the Sunlight Bar billboard.
Come nightfall, the glow of the streetlight casts their bodies
in a pleasing state. They know it and so they stand there,
smoking and laughing. Sometimes one can be heard to repeat a
conviction to the others. *I would never marry an old man*, she'll say.
What would you do if he's forcible? another will ask. *I would
rather smear human dung on my face than go with him*, is the answer.
Heh-heh, what if your own parents agree to the marriage?
Run away from home, my friend. And go where? *Wherever life
takes me.* They will stand there like that, waiting for what passes
for business around their parts – and I guess you know what that is.

Outside, inside

Here I am, on this frigid Saturday
in late 1998, kneading my eyes
and staring up a sloping Melindo
Street in Kamv'elihle. It's past
cockcrow. And raining – a gentle
shower, like baking flour off
a sieve. I go from the sidewalk
to the front stoep, then I am
at the window inside, watching
the mamas of the kitchens (damp
dresses and OK shopping bags as
bonnets) scamper past. Any time
now, I know Mama'll be walking
through the gate; she'll have her
nurse's cap. She'll be tired. She'll
be angry; there is nothing I can do.
So I make it to a bench near the
door to Madi's bedroom, and sit
down. On the carpet, there're the
blood drops – I'll tell Mama it was
Madi who started it, that I didn't
mean to. And then I'll make a
stubborn face; Mama'll shout that I
take off my pyjamas, find a washbowl
of water and pour Omo. And then –
then I'll rinse my hands clean.

Visitations

There is a story to be told
    about when he made it his business
to appear at my side at the post-match discourses
of what I would call my salad days.
    Albeit no courtesy tap on the shoulder
ever came, nor phlegm coaxed down the throat
to say *OK, son, I'm here*; there was only

the shadow of a beard on my face,
    and that defeated look of his I carry
when I am exhausted. This one time
I was running late for a kin's burial, not
    for the first time and the last yet. *I see
you have a question, Chief.* The hand-mirror
never lies, and I trust what my eyes saw.

One glass is what you promised yourself.
    But look now? It wasn't a question really,
hence I didn't do anything, save to rake
the brush over my head quietly, the way
he'd always done when we were preparing for church;
    the way he'd done on his last morning before
he got on the road and joined old man Magala.

Sons piggyback on their fathers.

Of course he was there, a removed audience
of my redemption songs from beyond the grave,
the way Kafka and his father continued to shadow-box,
long after they had quit staring at each other

at the dinner table. *"Everything was about you, father."*
"No. You are free, and that is why you are lost."

I guess we were happy

See how the grass grows, no matter
what? We grew up like that,
too.

also in the UHLANGA NEW POETS SERIES

Matric Rage by Genna Gardini (2015)

––––––––––––

also published by UHLANGA

the myth of this is that we're all in this together by Nick Mulgrew (2015)

uhlangapress.co.za

Printed in the United States
By Bookmasters